Human Anatomy Coloring Book

This book belongs to:

_____

AVID ANTS PRESS

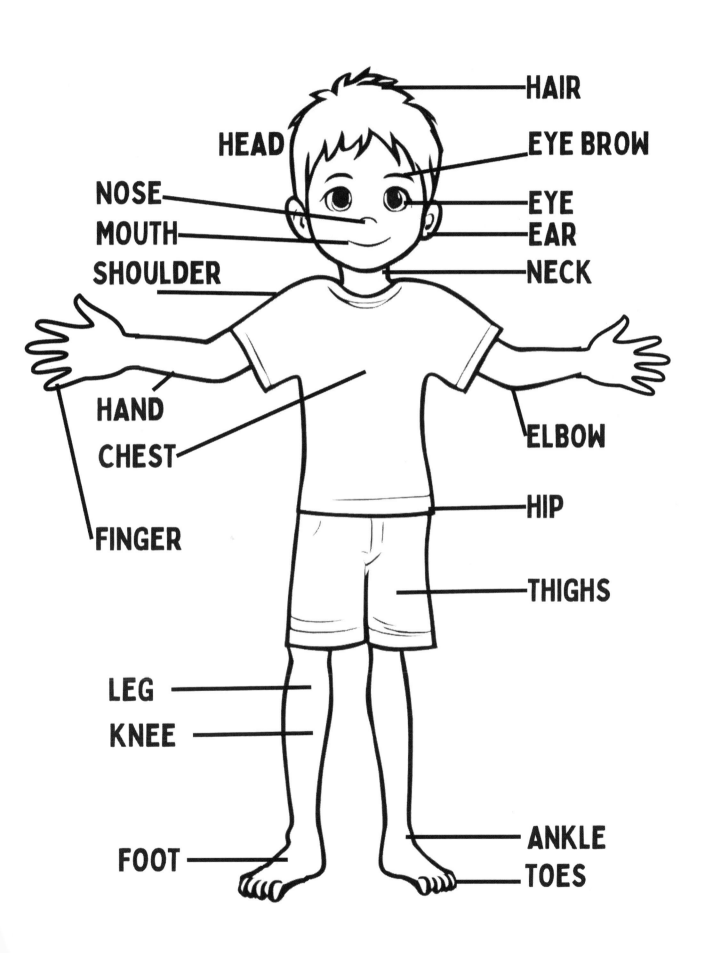

HAIR

HEAD

EYE BROW

NOSE

EYE

MOUTH

EAR

SHOULDER

NECK

HAND

ELBOW

CHEST

HIP

FINGER

THIGHS

LEG

KNEE

ANKLE

FOOT

TOES

EYES

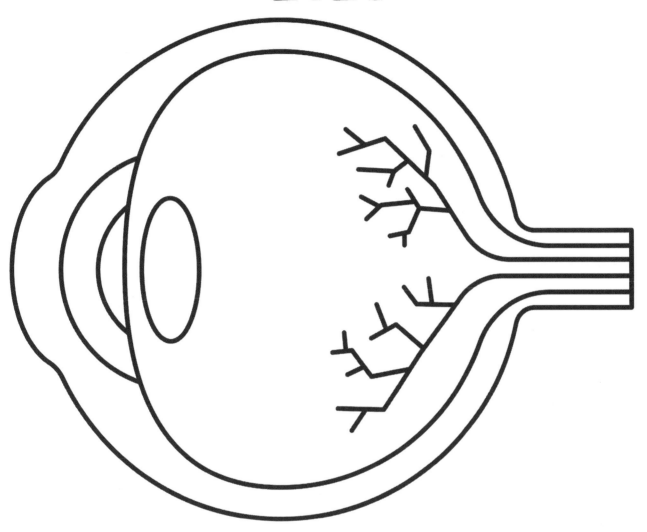

FUNCTION:

Your eyes are like cameras in your head. They help you see colors, shapes, and everything around you. Sight is one of our six senses.

CONTEXT:

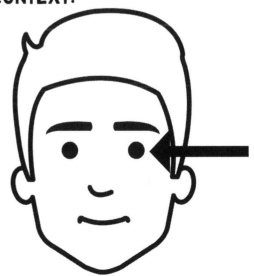

NOSE

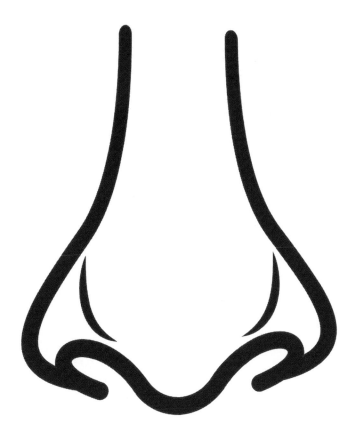

FUNCTION:

Your nose is like a tunnel for air. It lets air in for your lungs to breathe, like filling up a balloon. Tiny hairs inside the nose filters dust and germs, keeping your lungs clean. Your nose helps you smell everything too, like cookies baking or flowers blooming, and even tells you when your socks need a wash! So a nose can breathe, filter air and smell, all at a time.

CONTEXT:

EARS

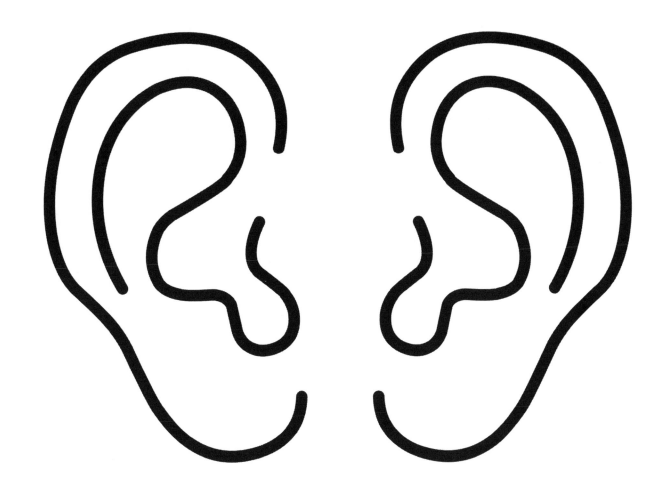

FUNCTION :

Your ears are like sound tunnels. They collect sounds with the floppy part outside, then send them through a long canal to your brain. Tiny bones inside the ear wiggle and make the sound louder. Finally, a special wire sends a message to your brain, telling you what you hear! Another function of ears is help you maintain your balance.

CONTEXT:

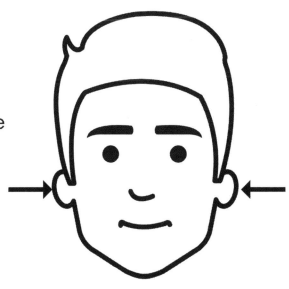

MOUTH

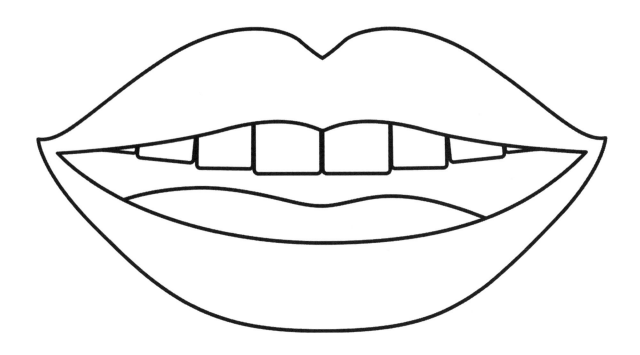

FUNCTION :

Your mouth has three major jobs.
Eating: To grind the food and swallow
Speaking : To produce different sounds
Tasting : To taste everything

CONTEXT:

TONGUE

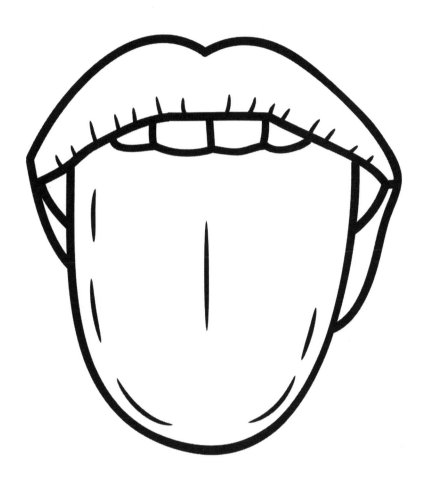

FUNCTION :

Your tongue helps you to talk. It also helps you to taste everything and move your food around in your mouth. Taste is one of our six senses.

CONTEXT:

TEETH

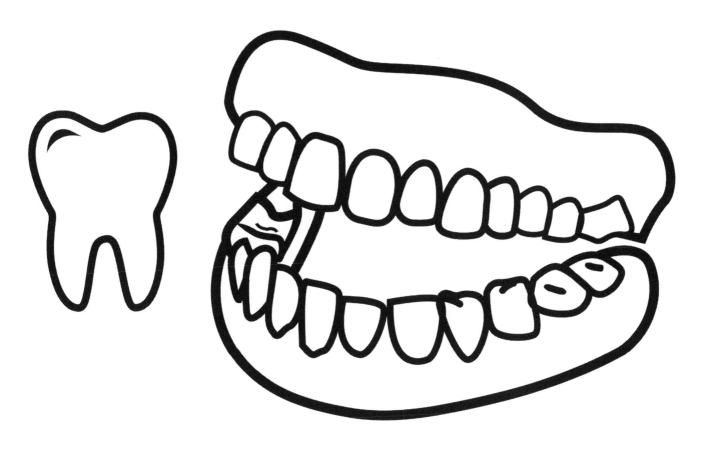

FUNCTION :

Teeth help to bite and chew your food, turning it into mush. This makes digestion easier for your stomach.

CONTEXT:

BRAIN

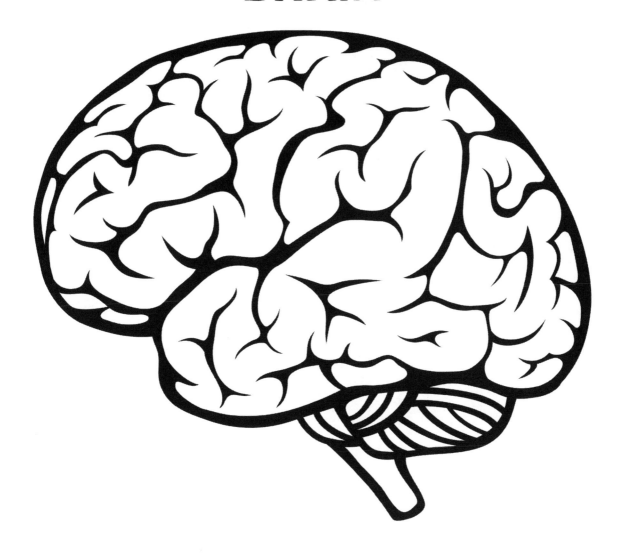

FUNCTION :

Your brain is the control center of your body, just like the captain of a ship! It sends messages to your muscles to move, tells your eyes what to see, even helps you dream. It controls your thoughts, memory and speech, arm and leg movements and the function of many organs within the body. It regulates how fast or slow your heart beats and lungs breathe as well.

CONTEXT:

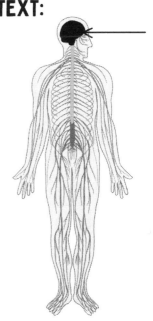

HEART

FUNCTION :

Your heart is kind of like a pump, or two pumps in one. It pumps blood around your body. Blood provides your body with the oxygen and nutrients it needs. It also carries away waste. Heart is part of body's circulatory system. It beats 60 to 100 times every minute. After delivering the oxygen, the blood returns to the heart. The heart then sends the blood to the lungs to pick up more oxygen.

CONTEXT:

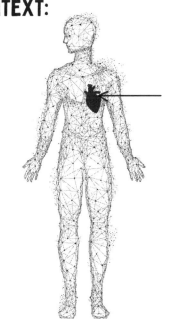

LUNGS

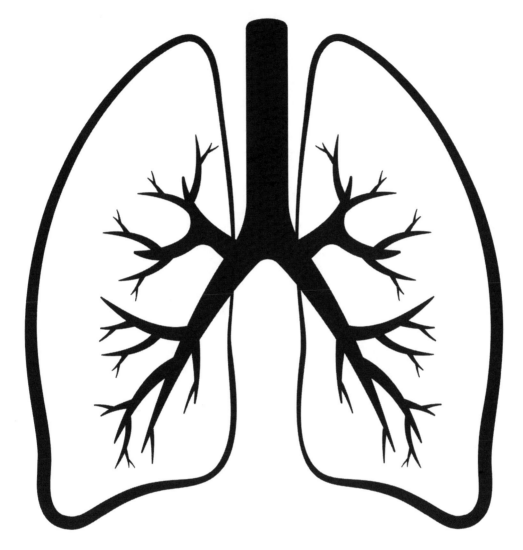

FUNCTION :

The lungs and respiratory system allow us to breathe. They bring oxygen into our bodies (called inspiration) and send carbon dioxide out (called expiration). This exchange of oxygen and carbon dioxide is called respiration. Respiration is the technical term for breathing.

CONTEXT:

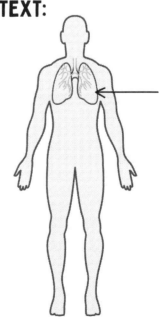

KIDNEYS

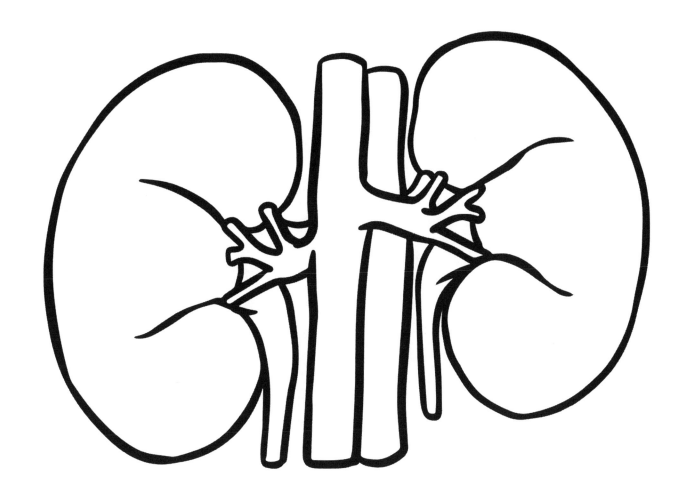

FUNCTION :

The most important job of the kidneys is to filter liquid waste from the blood and get rid of it in the form of urine. Kidneys are part of the body's urinary system. The kidneys produce urine to carry the liquid waste and extra fluid they have filtered out of your body.

CONTEXT:

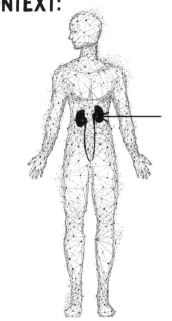

STOMACH

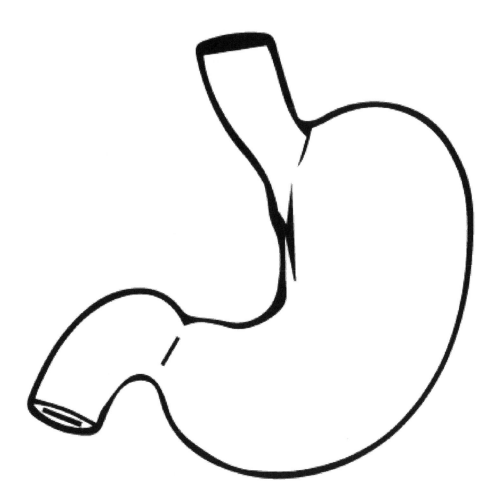

FUNCTION :

The stomach's main jobs are to store and break down food. The stomach churns and makes gastric juice to help digest the food we eat and protect us from germs. Food that has been broken down in the stomach is called chyme. The chyme is then passed on to the intestines for further break down.

CONTEXT:

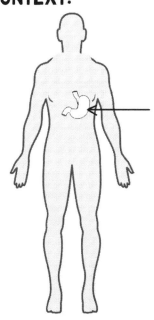

PANCREAS

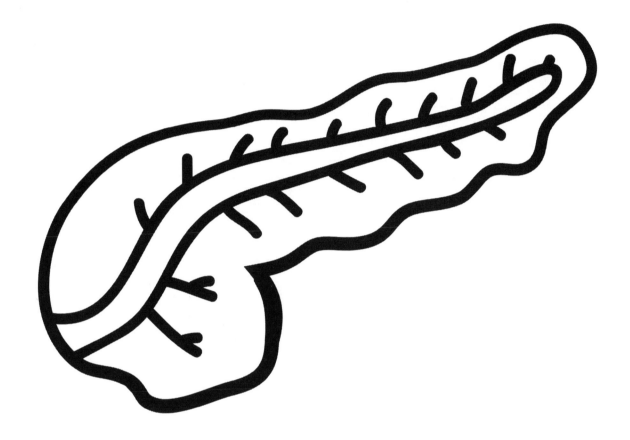

FUNCTION :

The pancreas is a long, flat gland in your belly. It sits behind the stomach and makes enzymes that are important for digestion. It also makes insulin and glucagon, which help control the sugar level in the blood.

CONTEXT:

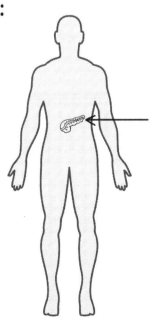

LIVER

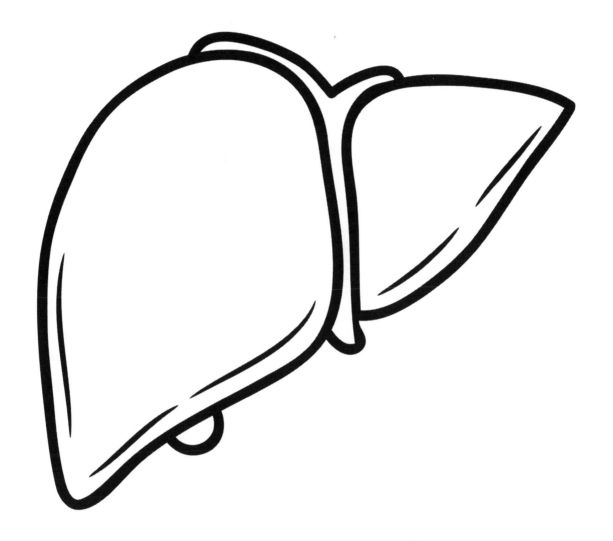

FUNCTION :

The major jobs of the liver are:
- It cleans your blood.
- It produces an important digestive liquid called bile aka bile juice.
- It stores energy in the form of a sugar called glycogen.

CONTEXT:

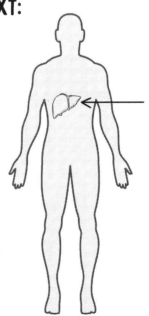

INTESTINE

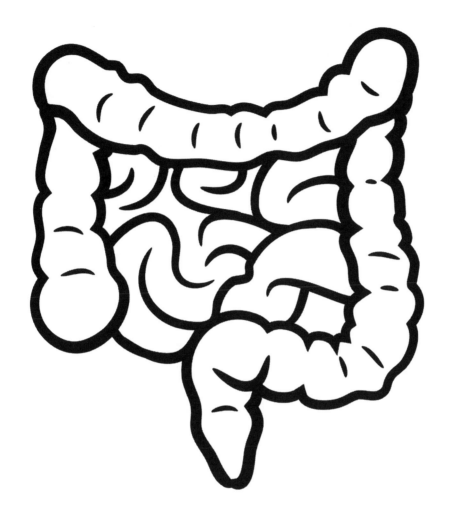

FUNCTION :

The intestines help in digestion by absorbing digested food materials for the body to turn it into energy. The food particles that are left after absorption is collected and converted into feces, or solid waste, for elimination.

CONTEXT:

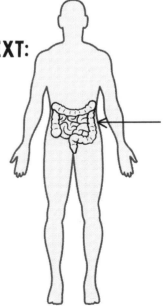

BLADDER

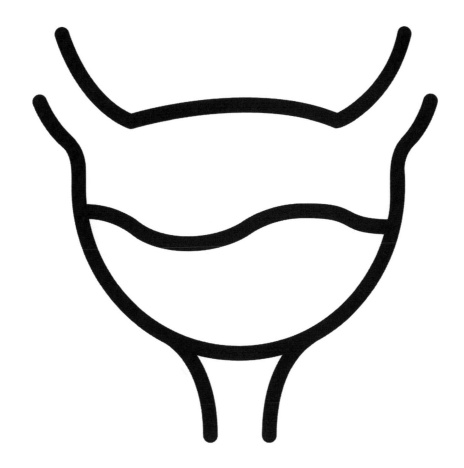

FUNCTION :

Bladder is a sac that holds pee until it's time to go to the bathroom.

CONTEXT:

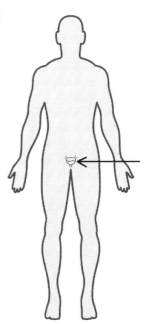

HAIR

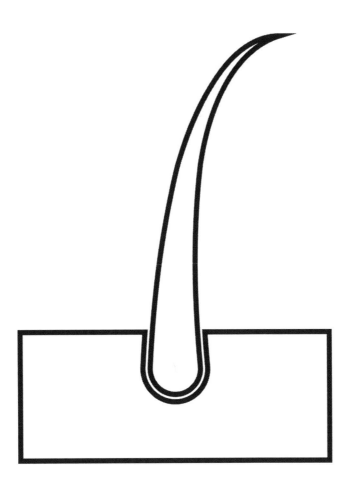

FUNCTION :

Depending on where the hair is, it has different jobs. Eyelashes protect your eyes by decreasing the amount of light and dust that go into them. The hair on your head keeps your head warm and provides a little cushioning for your skull. Eyebrows protect your eyes from sweat dripping down from your forehead. There's hair on almost every part of your body except lips, the palms of the hands, and the soles of the feet.

CONTEXT:

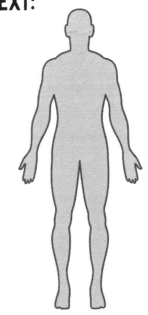

RED BLOOD CELL

FUNCTION :

Red blood cells (RBC) have the important job of carrying oxygen all over the body. These cells, which float in your blood, begin their journey in the lungs, where they pick up oxygen from the air you breathe. Then they travel to the heart, which pumps out the blood, delivering oxygen to all parts of your body. The red color of blood is because of these RBCs.

CONTEXT:

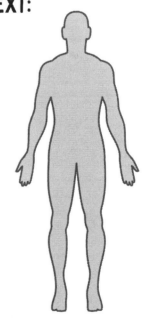

SPLEEN

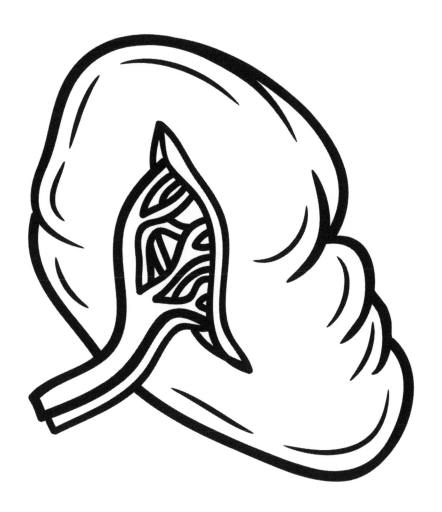

FUNCTION :

Spleen helps protect your body by destroying worn-out red blood cells and other foreign bodies (such as germs) from the bloodstream. The spleen is a part of the lymphatic system, which is an extensive drainage network.

CONTEXT:

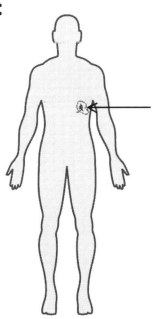

LARYNX

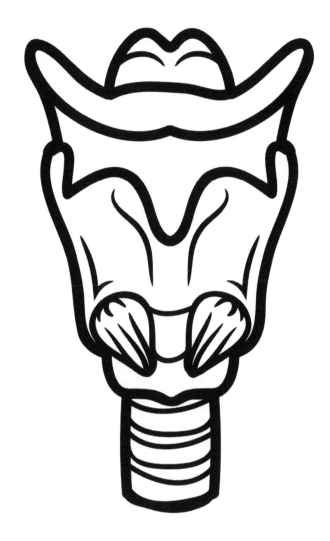

FUNCTION :

A larynx protects the food from entering the wind pipe while breathing. It also contains the vocal cords and works as a voice box for producing sounds for singing, talking, whistling, etc.,

CONTEXT:

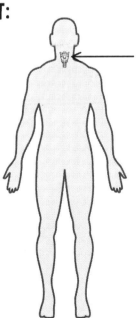

THYROID

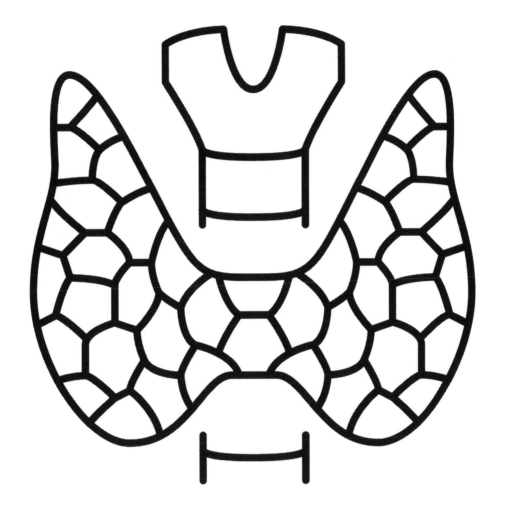

FUNCTION:

The job of the thyroid gland is to produce hormones that regulate the body's metabolic rate, development and growth. It plays a role in controlling heart, muscle and digestive functions, brain development and bone maintenance.

CONTEXT:

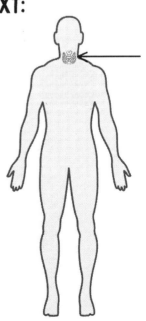

BONE

FUNCTION :

Your bones give your body its shape, and support and it protects your organs and systems.

CONTEXT:

BONE JOINT

FUNCTION :

Joints connect bones. They provide stability to the skeleton, and allow movement. They allow our bodies to move in many ways. Some joints open and close like a hinge (such as knees and elbows), whereas other joints allow for more complicated movement — a shoulder joint, for example, allows for backward, forward, sideways, and rotating movement.

CONTEXT:

RIB CAGE

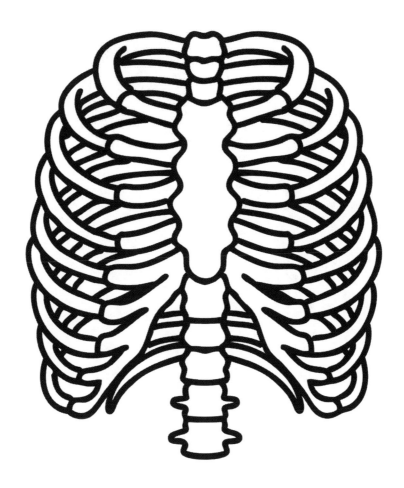

FUNCTION :

The rib cage surrounds the lungs and the
heart, serving as an vital means of bony
protection for these vital organs. It is made
up of rib bones that attach to the sternum
in front and the spine in the back.

CONTEXT:

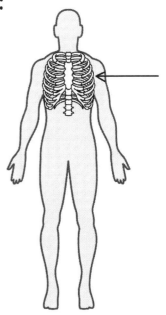

PELVIS

FUNCTION:

The pelvis aka pelvic bone acts as a tough ring of protection around parts of the digestive system, parts of the urinary system, and parts of the reproductive system

CONTEXT:

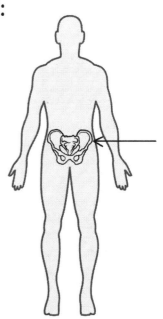

SPINE

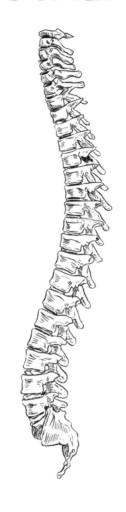

FUNCTION:

Spine runs the entire length of your neck and back. It has a unique design that allows us to move in all sorts of varied ways. Its main job is to support the body and provide protection for the spinal cord.

CONTEXT:

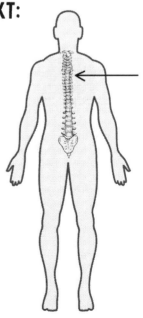

BONE MARROW

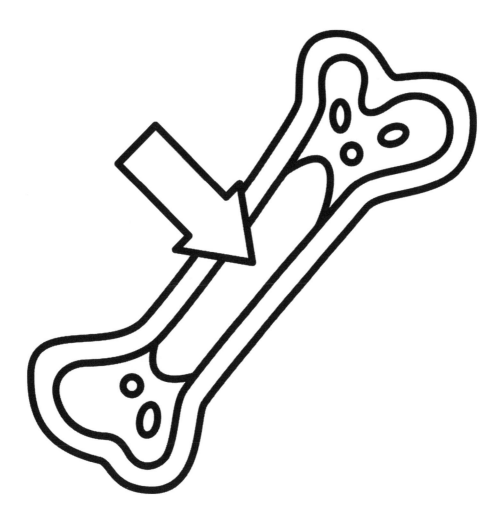

FUNCTION :

Bone marrow makes all kinds of blood cells like red blood cells that carry oxygen, white blood cells that fight infections, and platelets that help your blood clot. It produces and releases them into the blood stream.

CONTEXT:

NERVES

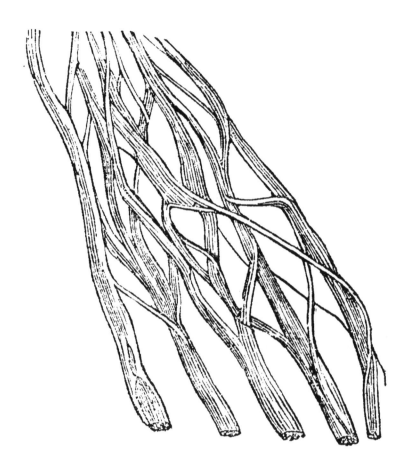

FUNCTION:

The job of the nerves is to carry information from brain to the other parts and vice versa. There are two main types of nerves: sensory nerves and motor nerves. Sensory nerves send information from the eyes, ears, mouth, nose, skin, and other body parts to the spinal cord and brain. Motor nerves carry messages in the other direction.

CONTEXT:

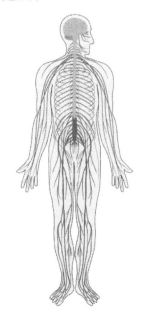

MUSCLES

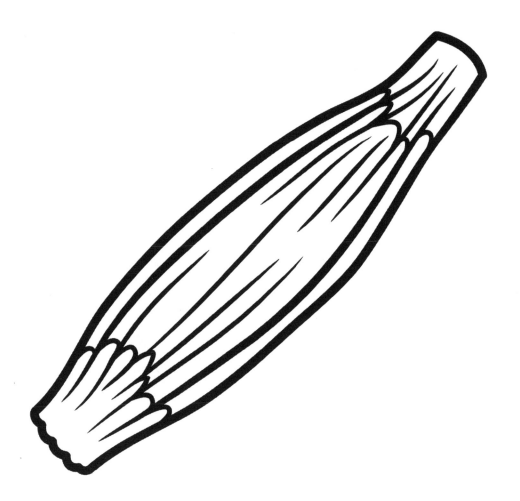

FUNCTION :

There are different types of muscles. Their job is to controls movement, posture (position of the body), and balance. They are present as layers or coverings of different organs that helps the organs work properly.

CONTEXT:

ARMS

FUNCTION :

Hands help us to do different actions as needed like pick, pinch, grasp, push, pull, carry, pat, scoop, etc.,

CONTEXT:

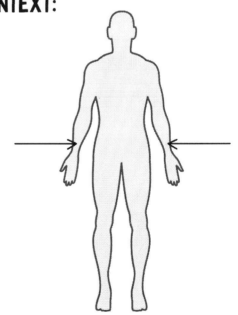

FINGERS

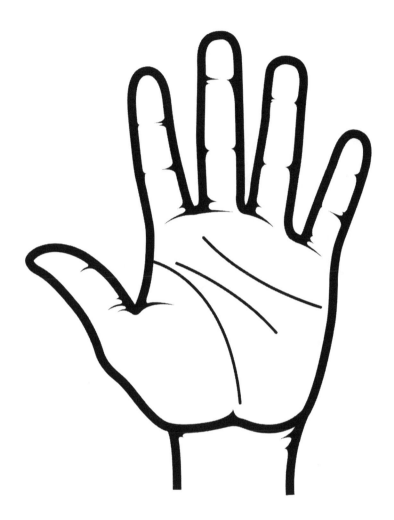

FUNCTION :

The five fingers are part of your hand and help in doing the different actions like pinch, grasp, pick, etc .,

CONTEXT:

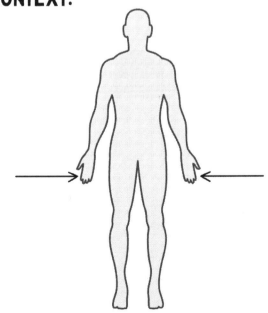

NAILS

FUNCTION :

Nails protect the tips of fingers and toes. It is made up of dead cells and so we don't feel any pain when the excess are clipped.

CONTEXT:

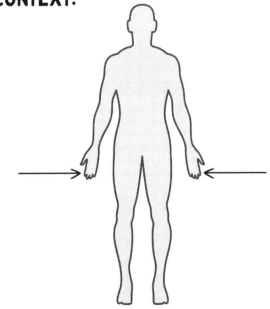

LEGS

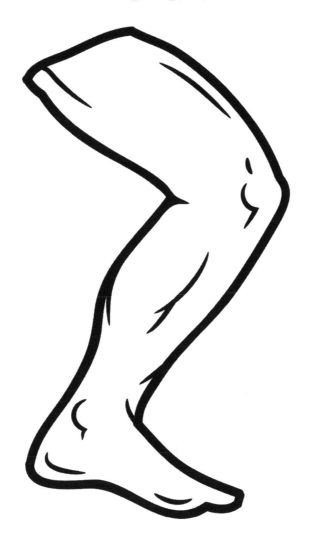

FUNCTION :

Legs support your body and help you move from one place to another. They help you to walk, run and jump

CONTEXT:

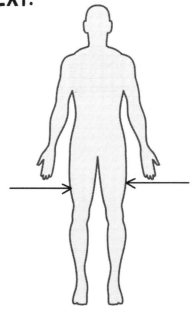

FEET

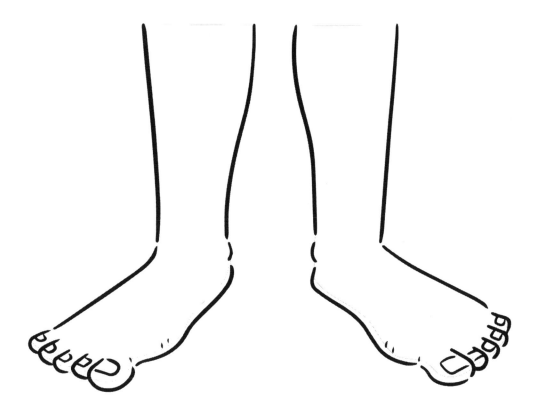

FUNCTION:

Feet are part of your legs. They support the weight of your body. They also help you to stand, walk, run and jump.

CONTEXT:

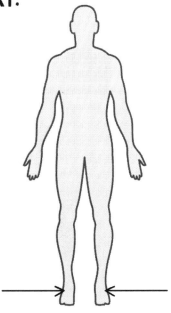

TOES

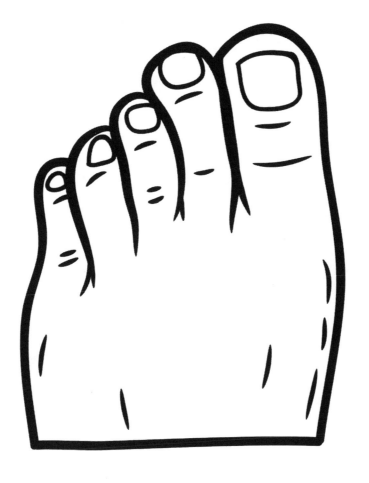

FUNCTION:

Toes along with other parts of the feet support the weight of your body. They also provide balance and absorb shocks while running, walking, or jumping.

CONTEXT:

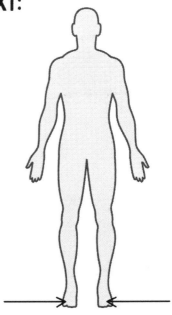

Made in United States
Orlando, FL
22 July 2024

49317936R00039